P9-ELT-485

FALL LEAVES CHANGE COLORS

KATHLEEN WEIDNER ZOEHFELD

SCHOLASTIC
REFERENCE

PHOTO CREDITS: Cover: Renee Lynn/Photo Researchers. Page 1: Willard Clay/Dembinsky Photo Associates; 3: Dan Dempster/DPA; 4: Richard Phelps Frieman/Photo Researchers; 5, 6: Adam Jones/DPA; 7: Randall B. Henne/DPA; 8: John Kaprielian/Photo Researchers; 9: Mark A. Schneider/DPA; 10: A. B. Sheldon/DPA; 11: David R. Frazier/Photo Researchers; 12–13: Jim Steinberg/Photo Researchers; 14: Willard Clay/DPA; 15: Rod Planck/DPA; 16–17: Eddie Hironaka/Image Bank; 18: Barb Gerlach/DPA; 19: Dan Dempster/DPA; 20: Michael P. Gadomski/Photo Researchers; 21: Mark E. Gibson/DPA; 22, 23: Adam Jones/DPA; 24: Michael Lustboder/Photo Researchers; 25: Jim Zipp/Photo Researchers; 26: Adam Jones/DPA; 27: Michael P. Gadomski/Photo Researchers; 28: Randall B. Henne/DPA; 29: Rod Planck/DPA; 30: Larry Ulrich/Tony Stone.

ISBN 0-439-26986-5

Book design by Barbara Balch and Kay Petronio
Photo research by Sarah Longacre

10 9 8 7 6 5 4 3   01 02 03 04

Printed in the U.S.A. 23

First printing, October 2001

We are grateful to Francie Alexander, reading specialist, and to Adele M. Brodkin, Ph.D., developmental psychologist, for their contributions to the development of this series.

Our thanks also to our science consultant Jim Sirch, Director of the Connecticut Audubon Center at Fairfield.

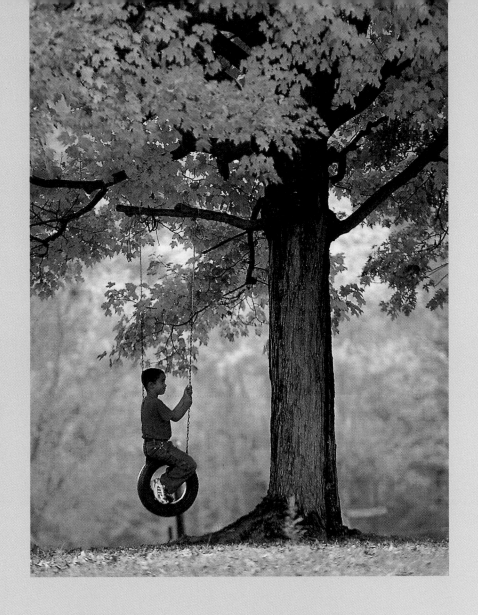

It's fall, and you can feel a
chill in the air. All around
you, the trees are beginning
to change.

In your backyard, in the park, and along country roads, trees are putting on their **autumn** (**aw**-tuhm) colors.

Their leaves are turning
yellow, orange, tan, and red.

In summer, most leaves are green. All summer long, something amazing is happening in those green leaves.

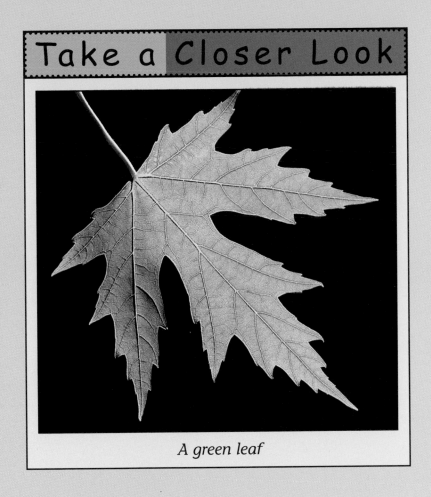

A green leaf

They are taking in sunshine, air, and water. And they are making food for the trees!

7

The green coloring in leaves is called **chlorophyll** (**klor**-uh-fil). Chlorophyll helps leaves take in light from the warm summer sun.

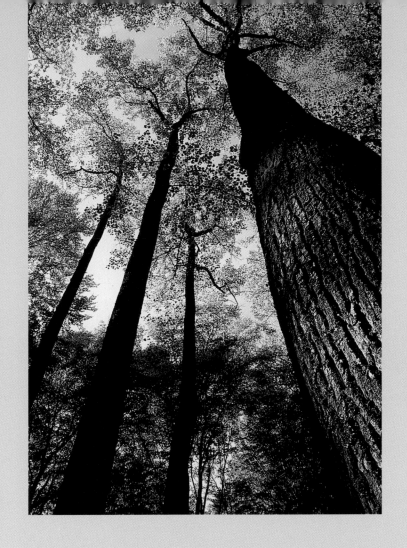

Leaves also have tiny openings for letting in air. From the air, leaves get a special gas called **carbon dioxide** (**car**-bun **deye**-ox-eyed).

After a rain, the trees' **roots**
take up water from the ground.
Water moves into the leaves.
Using light from the sun,
green leaves can turn water
and carbon dioxide into sugar.

The sugar moves from the leaves to all parts of the trees. Sugar is the special food that makes trees live and grow.

As summer ends, the days get shorter. The nights get longer. Autumn will soon be here.

Leaves get less and less light each day. This tells the trees that it is time to stop making food. The leaves begin to die.

13

The chlorophyll in the
leaves fades away, and their
color changes.

A leaf that is beginning to change color

Each leaf loses its green coloring slowly.

As the chlorophyll fades, other colors in the leaf begin to show.

The leaves of some trees
turn yellow or orange.

16

These colors are in the leaves
all summer. But the strong green
of the chlorophyll hides them.

The leaves of other trees
turn red or purple.

Sunny days and cool autumn nights make the sugar in the leaves turn red or purple. As the green coloring in the leaves fades, the color of the sugar shows through.

A few types of trees
have leaves that turn
brown or tan.

In these leaves, a coloring
called **tannin** shows as their
green coloring fades.

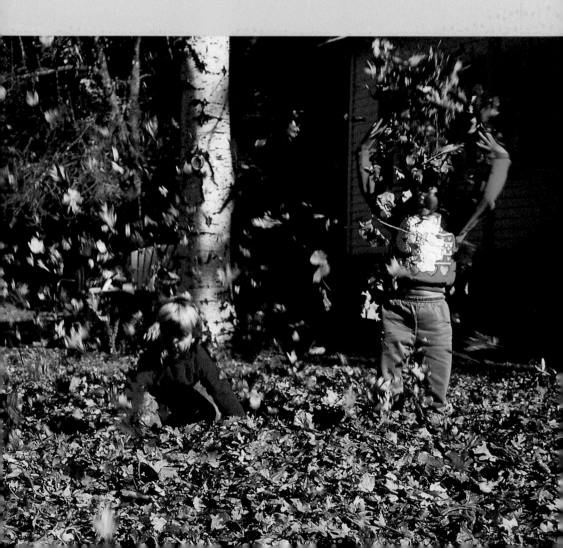

Take a Closer Look

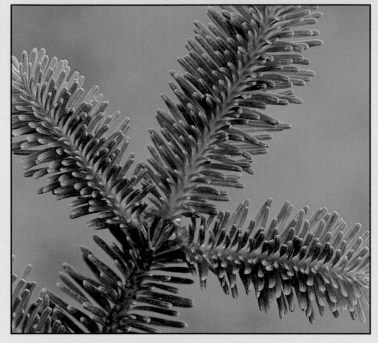

Evergreen needles

Trees whose leaves stay green all year are called evergreens. Most evergreens have tough, narrow leaves called needles.

22

Evergreens shed their needles only a few at a time. Trees whose leaves change color lose *all* their leaves in autumn.

As a leaf dies, the part
of the stem that holds it to
its branch gets weak.

Take a Closer Look

The weakening stem of a leaf

24

Chilly autumn winds
make many leaves fly from
their branches. Heavy rains
make others fall.

25

Under your feet, the ground
is covered with a patchwork of
beautiful colors.

26

Over your head, the branches look dark and bare. The trees are ready for their winter rest.

Tiny buds line the branches
where the leaves once were.

The buds are tough enough
to stand the frosty winter.

Take a Closer Look

Buds at the tip of a branch

The buds protect the new green leaves that will unfold in spring.

Glossary

autumn (aw-tuhm)—one of the four seasons. Autumn comes after summer and before winter. It is also called fall.

carbon dioxide (**car**-bun **deye**-ox-eyed)—one of the main gases in the air.

chlorophyll (**klor**-uh-fil)—the green coloring found in the leaves of most plants.

roots—the part of a plant that grows under the ground.

tannin—a tan-colored material found in the bark, leaves, roots, and fruits of some plants.

A Note to Parents

Learning to read is such an exciting time in a child's life. You may delight in sharing your favorite fairy tales and picture books with your child.

But don't forget the importance of introducing your child to the world of nonfiction. The ability to read and comprehend factual material will be essential to your child in school, and throughout life. The Scholastic Science Readers™ series was created especially with beginning readers in mind. These books, with their clear texts and beautiful photographs, will help you to share the wonders of science with *your* new reader.

Suggested Activity

Help your child create his or her own autumn leaf album. Go on a walk in a park or wooded area together and collect leaves of every shape, size, and color. Slide your leaves between the pages of a heavy book for a few days to press them. When your leaves are flattened, you can use the Internet or nature guide books to find names for the leaves you've found (oak, birch, sassafras, etc.). With tape or glue, mount your leaves on colorful construction paper and make a label for each. Your child can create a cover for the album with markers or crayons. Using staples or a hole punch and yarn, bind the pieces of paper together to form a book. You've created a reminder of fall that you can enjoy all year round!